Hugo Joins the Band

By Cameron Macintosh

It was Big Band Day
at Dash and Hugo's school.

Bands sang and played
for the students.

Dash got up and sang
with her pop band.

The students loved it!

"I want to be in a band, too,"
Hugo said.
"I can play the tuba!"

Hugo went to chat with Dash.

Dash, can I play the tuba in your pop band?

"A tuba would not fit in my band," said Dash.

"What can I play?" said Hugo.

"Can you get a flute?" said Dash.

At home, Hugo went to Mum's big shed.

He picked up a long tin tube.

"This tin tube could be a flute!" Hugo said.

"Mum!" Hugo yelled.

"Can you drill into this tube?"

Mum got her drill and drilled
into the tin tube.

"Thanks, Mum!" said Hugo.
"The tube is a flute!"

Hugo played and played
his tin flute.

Then he played his flute
for Dash.

"Your flute is good!"
said Dash.
"You can be in my band!"

"Thanks, Dash!" said Hugo.
"Let's play!"

CHECKING FOR MEANING

1. Which instrument did Hugo want to play in the band at first? *(Literal)*

2. What did Mum have to do to make the tin tube into a flute? *(Literal)*

3. Why did Hugo have to play and play his tin flute? *(Inferential)*

EXTENDING VOCABULARY

students	What are *students*? How many students are in your class?
flute	How do you play a *flute*? How can you make different sounds?
tube	What shape is a *tube*? What things do you know that can be in a tube?

MOVING BEYOND THE TEXT

1. Which instruments are often played in a band?

2. Instruments can be grouped into strings, woodwind, brass and percussion. Which groups do the tuba and the flute belong to?

3. Talk about other instruments that can be played by covering the holes with your fingers.

4. What do you need to do to learn how to play a musical instrument? How often should you practise? How can you share music with your family?

SPELLINGS FOR THE LONG /u/ VOWEL SOUND

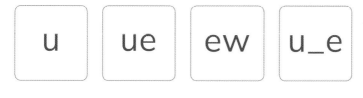

u   ue   ew   u_e

PRACTICE WORDS

students

Hugo's

Hugo

flute

tuba

tube